# FRAMEWORK PROFESSIONAL DEVELOPMENT:

## Self-study Modules for Teachers and Lecturers

## DEVELOP YOUR CLASSROOM CONTROL AND DISCIPLINE

**Roger Smith**

Framework Press Educational Publishers Ltd.
Parkfield
Greaves Road
LANCASTER
LA1 4TZ

First published 1996

ISBN 1 85008 132 8

**FRAMEWORK PROFESSIONAL DEVELOPMENT:**
**Self-study Modules for Teachers and Lecturers**
**DEVELOP YOUR CLASSROOM CONTROL**
**AND DISCIPLINE**

© Roger Smith

The right of Roger Smith to be identified as author of this work has been asserted by him in accordance with the Copyright, Designs and Patents Act 1988

A catalogue record for the book is available from the British Library

All rights reserved

Typeset by AMA Graphics Ltd., Preston

Printed in Great Britain
by The Charlesworth Group, Huddersfield

Cover design by John Angus
Illustrations by Trevor Green

# Table of Contents

## The Author:

Roger Smith has worked in schools, a college of Further Education, the Open University and the University of Warwick. He has taught INSET courses, published widely and broadcast on BBC Radio. Seven photocopiable packs have been published by Framework Press: *The Effective School, Volume 1: Teachers Working Together: The Whole School Approach* (1990); *The Effective School, Volume 2: Classroom Techniques and Management* (1990); *The Heads' and Deputies' Handbook: Managing Schools in the 1990s* (1992); *Managing Pupil Behaviour in School and Classroom: In-house Training Materials for Teachers* (1993); *Preparing for Appraisal: Self-evaluation for Teachers in Primary and Secondary Schools* (1993); *Preparing for Inspection: The Whole School Approach* (1994) and *Managing Your Classroom: A Guide to Better Teaching* (1994). In this series of handbooks, he has produced *Develop Your Classroom Management Skills* (1995) and *Preparing Yourself for Inspection* (1995). As the Headteacher of a large Combined School, he has been involved in many committees and planning groups. He also works in the Education Department of the University of Warwick.

## Editor:

Karen Westall

## Acknowledgements:

The author would like to thank the many people who have contributed directly and indirectly to the thinking that has culminated in this book, especially all those colleagues, tutors, teachers, course and conference members who have helped, often without knowing, to shape the ideas expressed here. He also wishes to thank particularly his wife, children and friends for their support.

# Introduction

Since the Education Reform Act of 1988, teachers have found themselves having to come to terms with the changing content of the National Curriculum, rather than having time to think constructively about the maintenance of classroom control and discipline. Reports in the *Times Educational Supplement* and concerns expressed by most teachers' unions over the increase in numbers of disruptive pupils have, however, made it essential to develop assertive and appropriate classroom management skills, because, without them, the delivery of the subject content will be less effective than it should be.

All teachers have a fund of skills, expertise and knowledge and thinking about which of these work and why they work will help you to maintain your skills and develop new ones in a more focused way. Skilled teachers can make discipline and classroom management look easy, but even experienced teachers can meet difficult and challenging classes. Even in well-motivated and happy class there can be individual pupils who pose challenging discipline problems for the teacher.

This handbook has been written for teachers who are concerned about the seeming increase in the number of behaviour problems of their pupils and it will help every teacher develop new skills and refine and increase the usefulness of old techniques.

When you work through the Units, it is important that you think about your own teaching in your own school. After all, the handbook has been written to help you improve your practice. There are Activities dealing with how to manage individual pupils, how to set behaviour targets, how you, as a teacher, remain in control, how to begin lessons successfully and how to establish working rules and relationships. If you are able to think carefully about all these areas and, where possible, discuss them with a colleague, you will learn from your mistakes and be able to build on your many successes.

## UNIT 1

# Managing the Individual Pupil

Inappropriate pupil behaviour by an individual is often the cause of incidents that disrupt the rights of other pupils. If this happens, the majority of a class or teaching group will find it difficult, if not impossible to learn.

Managing groups of pupils so that this kind of activity is reduced to a minimum is neither easy nor based on a few simple guidelines. Pupils who behave badly usually have a low sense of self-esteem. Teachers, who have to deal with the problems of such pupils on a daily basis, may also have a sense of being de-skilled because of the difficulties and demands put upon them. This Unit looks at various approaches that should reduce disruption and, therefore, improve the quality of teaching and learning.

In B. Rogers, *You Know the Fair Rule* (Longman, 1991), three basic types of discipline are suggested:

✤ *Preventative discipline*: This is where there has been careful planning in terms of rules, classroom organisation and consequences of disruption.

✤ *Corrective discipline*: This is where the teacher corrects the disruptive behaviour in some way.

✤ *Supportive discipline*: This is where the corrective side of the process of discipline is supported by follow-up work, so that supportive relationships are rebuilt and re-established.

If you are to be successful, you must be able to recognise and use all three methods.

It is no good just correcting pupils over and over again without being able to work within a preventative ethos where support for the individual is the norm.

Your classroom discipline and control has to be seen to be fair to all your pupils. It has to decrease rather than increase hostility and improve the working atmosphere of the classroom.

# ◆ ACTIVITY 1.1 ◆◆◆

This Activity provides a list of useful teaching skills which you can use in your classroom when you are managing difficult and challenging pupils. The skills, however, are not just useful when there are difficulties. They are really good skills to have and use all the time.

Read through each statement and tick the appropriate box, indicating how often you use this skill.

In the final column write P if you think that the statement is PREVENTATIVE DISCIPLINE, C if you think it is CORRECTIVE and S if you think it is SUPPORTIVE.

*Create an attractive and welcoming classroom environment.*

## Effective Classroom Management Skills

| An effective teacher can . . . | *Not often* | *Often* | *Very often* | *Type of discipline* |
|---|---|---|---|---|
| 1. . . . organise the curriculum to cater for pupils of different abilities | | | | |
| 2. . . . ignore in a tactful way some kinds of disruptive behaviour | | | | |
| 3. . . . give pupils choices that they are able to cope with | | | | |
| 4. . . . find time to follow up behaviour problems and disruption later, after the initial trauma has subsided | | | | |
| 5. . . . build up a positive ethos in the classroom | | | | |
| 6. . . . create an attractive and welcoming classroom environment | | | | |
| 7. . . . recognise the importance of knowing what to say and how to say it when dealing with a pupil who is off-task and disruptive | | | | |
| 8. . . . make available good, relevant and adequate resources | | | | |
| 9. . . . create space for, and know when to deal with, pupils by removing them from friends and from the classroom | | | | |
| 10. . . . use different kinds of questioning both to elicit information and solve problems | | | | |

| | | | | | |
|---|---|---|---|---|---|
| 11. | . . . give simple, effective and formal warnings | | | | |
| 12. | . . . encourage pupils, often by praising and being enthusiastic about their achievements | | | | |
| 13. | . . . develop an ethos where respect for everyone is the norm | | | | |
| 14. | . . . plan the classroom in terms of seating, access to seats and equipment, tidiness, etc. | | | | |
| 15. | . . . develop a work-orientated classroom with very clear expectations about tasks and outcomes, i.e. what is expected at the end of a period of time | | | | |
| 16. | . . . use all kinds of techniques, including separating culprits from their peers and disciplining them alone | | | | |
| 17. | . . . quickly re-establish a good relationship with a pupil who has been disciplined | | | | |
| 18. | . . . use other colleagues to help solve problems | | | | |
| 19. | . . . frequently stop pupils and remind them of stated and/or agreed classroom rules | | | | |
| 20. | . . . spot incidents coming and defuse situations | | | | |
| 21. | . . . work out long-term systems such as pupil-teacher contracts | | | | |

## ◆ **ACTIVITY 1.2** ◆◆◆

When you have finished your *Effective classroom management skills* chart, try and answer the following questions. There are spaces for you to write down your ideas and notes.

| |
|---|
| 1. Think of an individual pupil whom you teach. What will be the consequences of not being able to provide PREVENTATIVE discipline? |
| 2. Why is the ability to use CORRECTIVE discipline essential if you are aiming to be an effective teacher? |
| 3. Why is it necessary to act in a SUPPORTIVE way with some of your individual pupils? |

In *Activity 1.1*, Numbers 1, 3, 6, 8, 9, 10, 14, 15 were PREVENTATIVE DISCIPLINE 2, 7, 11, 16, 19, 20 were CORRECTIVE and 4, 5, 12, 13, 17, 18, 21 were SUPPORTIVE.

You should have a spread of ticks in the *Very often* column.

◆ **ACTIVITY 1.3** ◆◆◆

Remember, this Unit is concentrating on the individual pupil. When you are finding certain pupils challenging and difficult to manage, it should be possible to suggest how the discipline techniques in *Activity 1.1* could be used. In other words, there should be a route through the three types of discipline.

Let's see if you can do this.

First of all, describe a disruptive incident involving an individual pupil that has happened in your classroom recently. Use the space to describe it in reasonable detail. It will help if you can think of an incident that you handled badly.

| *Disruptive incident*: |
|---|
| |

Now use the *Action route* below to plot how you could stop the incident happening. The route itself is only a series of quite bare statements. You have to add what you would do. It describes a sequence of actions and stays the same, but what you do depends on the disruptive situation.

After each stage, write down what you would do for the situation you have described. It is important to be honest, because only by being truthful will you be able to learn from mistakes and build on successes.

## Action Route for Classroom Disruption

| |
|---|
| **Stage 1:**<br>This is the stage when the disruptive incident first occurs.<br>*Action to be taken*:<br>Ignore the incident unless it is endangering another pupil or causing intense distress to someone else. |
| **Stage 2:**<br>You cannot ignore the behaviour by this particular pupil, or, if you have ignored it, you find that it has happened again.<br>*Action to be taken*:<br>1.  Give an instruction or make a direct statement. |
| What exactly would you say or do for the example you have described? |

2. You could repeat a rule or remind the pupil involved of a rule.

---

What rule would you have created to try to avoid what you have described happening?

---

How would you remind the pupil? What would you say? Where would you stand?

---

3. You could question the pupil and gain some kind of feedback as to the state of mind, motives, etc.

---

What kinds of questions would you ask and how would you ask them?

---

**Stage 3:**
The steps you have taken in *Stage 2* have not been totally effective and after a period of time the incident has occurred again.
*Action to be taken*:
1. Repeat *Stage 2*.

2.  Give the pupil a clear choice. In other words, you are issuing a threat that you are able and willing to carry out. The threat or choice you are giving will be along the lines of: 'If you do that again, this will happen to you.'

How will you give the choice? Where will you be? What will you be doing?

What choices will you offer? What threats can you, and are you, willing to make?

## Stage 4:

The behaviour persists and you have to take final action.
*Action to be taken*:
Carry out the threats.

What sanctions are you going to impose?

How are you going to carry out your threats?

**Stage 5:**
This takes place when the incident is over and after you have dealt with the immediate problem. There has to be a return to some kind of reasonable relationship. If this doesn't happen, the atmosphere and ethos of the classroom will suffer.

How do you achieve this?

♦ ACTIVITY 1.4 ♦♦♦

By doing *Activity 1.3* thoughtfully and honestly, you should have greater insights into the approach you could adopt when confronted by a disruptive incident in your classroom. Now you have to develop your techniques even further.

To do this successfully, you will have to plan your approach because, if you use the wrong method, it could result in the incident getting out of hand and escalating into further problems and confrontations.

You must be able to recognise that when disruption occurs you have to do or say something. In other words, you will have to take decisions. What you do should not be a 'knee-jerk' reaction, but should be as considered and as purposeful as any other aspect of classroom planning and management.

In this Activity, there are several incidents. After each one, decide what you might say to the pupil and how you might say it.

Write your responses in the spaces.

When you have done this, *and not before*, look at the next section of the Activity. Two alternative examples of what might be said to try to solve the problem created by each of the eight incidents are given.

Underneath each one decide what might happen if you used this way of talking and acting.

When you have completed this, *and not before*, move on to Activity 1.5.

## Incident 1

A girl has committed a minor error by not ruling a margin on a piece of work that is going to be used for assessment.

What would you do and say?

## Incident 2

A boy has snatched a text book out of the hand of a girl at the next desk.

What would you do and say?

## Incident 3

Two boys are discussing what they are going to do in the evening instead of doing the work that has been set.

What would you do and say?

## Incident 4

A boy runs into the classroom, lightly punches a friend on the shoulder and knocks some work off another pupil's desk.

What would you do and say?

## Incident 5

During a technology lesson two boys have used a glue gun to stick a girl's ruler and pencil to the floor.

> What would you do and say?

## Incident 6

A girl swears loudly and obscenely during a quiet period when everyone else in the class is working.

> What would you do and say?

## Incident 7

Again in technology, a boy in a group is hammering a screw into a piece of wood. The other two membrs of the group are very displeaed with him.

> What would you do and say?

## Incident 8

In the middle of a lesson, a girl playfully pushes another girl against a desk which knocks over some paint.

> What would you do and say?

Make sure that you have finished this before you move on to the next section.

*The paint gets knocked over.*

As you read the two alternatives below for each incident, you may find that you are assuming that one alternative is always correct. Is it?

Write very careful notes in the consequences spaces below each one.

---

**Incident 1**: *Alternative A*
'Look! I have told you time and time again that you need a margin on every piece of work. I'm not paid to keep telling you this every single day.'
(Voice rising) 'Now do it properly!'

What are the consequences of using this alternative?

*Alternative B*
(Quiet voice) 'Look! You've forgotten something on this page.'

What are the consequences of using this alternative?

**Incident 2**: *Alternative A*
(Voice loud at first and rising) 'Don't snatch at things like that. You are a real little animal, aren't you? What are you doing?'

What are the consequences of using this alternative?

*Alternative B*
(Very firm but very controlled voice) 'When she has finished using the book, I am sure that you will be able to borrow it. Until then, you will have to wait.'

What are the consequences of using this alternative?

**Incident 3**: *Alternative A*
(Voice loud and harsh) 'Look! I'm absolutely fed up. You aren't working, you are just messing about and gossiping. You are wasting my time. Now you move over there and you get out of the room. Go on, move!'

What are the consequences of using this alternative?

*Alternative B*

'Come on, you two, keep the noise down, thanks. We're all trying to work here.' (This type of gossiping is often extremely interesting and important to those taking part and is likely to continue, so repeat what you have just said and continue) 'OK! You two, I've reminded you of the rules about working noise. If you can't keep to them, you'll have to work separately and on your own.'

What are the consequences of using this alternative?

**Incident 4**: *Alternative A*

(Shouting) 'I must have told you millions of times about coming into the classroom like that. Don't ever do it again.'

What are the consequences of using this alternative?

*Alternative B*

(Calmly reminding a pupil of an important rule) 'Remember, don't come into the classroom like that. It's a really important rule for everyone.'

What are the consequences of using this alternative?

**Incident 5**: *Alternative A*
(Voice loud and rather ranting) 'What do you think you are doing messing about with that glue gun. If you can't use it properly, don't use it at all.' (Voice rising even further) 'Do you understand?'

What are the consequences of using this alternative?

*Alternative B*
'I am sorry but I regard that as a serious misuse of tools. Go and wait outside Mrs Halliday's office and we will both speak to you during break.'

What are the consequences of using this alternative?

**Incident 6**: *Alternative A*
'Hey you! Don't you dare say that again.' (More loudly) 'I don't think I have ever heard anything so disgusting. Come here immediately! . . . Now I don't care how you are allowed to speak at home, but don't think you can get away with that kind of language here.'

What are the consequences of using this alternative?

*Alternative B*
(Very firm with full eye contact from fairly close range) 'I want to see you straight away. There are strict rules about swearing and you know that.'

What are the consequences of using this alternative?

**Incident 7**: *Alternative A*
(Lots of sighs and a touch of sarcasm) 'Look at that screw head. I must have shown you a thousand times how to use a screw driver. What am I supposed to do, let one of the girls do it? . . . Give it me! Pass me the screwdriver. Now watch what I am doing and you might get better in a few years' time.'

What are the consequences of using this alternative?

*Alternative B*
(With smiles and perhaps a pat on the shoulder for other members of the group to indicate support) 'Well, you are certainly making a mess of that. Here's how you must do it in future. Now let me see you using the tools properly.' (Watches him do the job properly)

What are the consequences of using this alternative?

**Incident 8**: *Alternative A*
(Shouting desperately) 'Just look at what you've done! Look at the mess! . . . Go on look at it! What do you think you are doing you stupid girl? Go and find something to clear it up and don't think you will be playing hockey for the school this week!'

What are the consequences of using this alternative?

*Alternative B*
(Calmly) 'That's a terrible mess isn't it? Let's see if we can clear it up and then we can talk about how to avoid it happening again.'

What are the consequences of using this alternative?

# ◆ ▨ ACTIVITY 1.5 ◆◆◆

When you have finished *Activity 1.4*, it is worth spending some time thinking about how you have responded to each incident, including both my alternatives and their consequences.

You should not be thinking in terms of 'right' and 'wrong', but rather in terms of the consequences of using a particular response.

*Alternative A*s were all rather rushed and probably thoughtless, spur-of-the-moment reactions. *Alternative B*s were much more thoughtful responses.

In other words, they were more planned, organised and less rushed.

What do you think the consequences will be of rushed knee-jerk reactions?

What are the consequences of a more rational, balanced response?

◆ **ACTIVITY 1.6** ◆◆◆

Dealing with individual pupils who are challenging and disruptive is often a matter of having the right repertoire of skills. In fact, many of the ideas in this handbook are based on the idea that teaching skills can be learned and developed.

This Activity suggests some common, and possibly well-known, skills of control. Whether they are or not, it is still important to recognise them as fundamental teaching skills.

Not only will they help you deal with individual pupils but they will have a *ripple effect*. This means that, when you are dealing with a particular problem caused by a particular pupil, it will be recognised by other pupils and affect how they get on with their work.

Most of the following *Control tactics* are useful within the following guidelines:

✤ If you threaten pupils, make sure that you intend to carry out the threat.
✤ If you have to take action to stop an incident, always make sure that the action you take is at the lowest possible level. Save your 'big guns' for really serious occasions.
✤ Try to make sure that there is some kind of rule that covers most eventualities, so that you have to make fewer *ad hoc* decisions.

It is important that you use some, if not all, of the control tactics, either on their own or linked together.

It is equally important to be aware that pupils at certain ages will react differently to some of the control skills. In fact, there are some that will have a very negative effect if used with older pupils who are likely to be disruptive and prone to wanting some kind of confrontation.

For example, touch can be very counter-productive with older pupils. It can be given different meanings by both girls and boys. It may also be an invasion of personal space, which, in many adolescent cultures, is a signal for confrontation.

Read each of the following tactics.

## Control Tactics

*Non-verbal control tactics*

1. Using eye contact
2. Raising the eyebrow during eye contact
3. Frowning
4. Giving a filthy look
5. Shaking your head whilst doing any combination of Numbers 1–4
6. Pointing a finger at the same time as doing any combination of Numbers 1–5
7. Smiling *not* at the same time as any of Numbers 2–6
8. Using a calming gesture with your hands at the same time as a smile
9. Nodding at the same time as smiling
10. Using a quiet gesture of finger on lips on its own and with Numbers 1, 2, 3 or 8

*Sound as a control tactic.*

*Sound as a control tactic*

1. Clapping hands
2. Tapping on the desk with a hard object or closing door loudly
3. Snapping fingers
4. Calling someone's name
5. Coughing
6. Using a starting signal such as 'Right, everyone ready?' at the same time as any combination of Numbers 1–5

*Contact as a control tactic*

1. Sitting next to a pupil
2. Standing next to a pupil
3. Using a calming gesture of a hand on the shoulder
4. Walking towards a pupil purposefully
5. Removing an object that is causing a problem
6. Placing hand on arm and leading the pupil somewhere else

NB. There are *very* important issues related to touching pupils in any kind of way. You must use your own judgement regarding such tactics as a hand on an arm or shoulder. My advice would be, if in doubt, *don't touch*.

Finally, it is important to try and reflect on some of the aspects of this Unit.

Use the spaces to respond to the following questions:

What are your *four* most difficult kinds of disruption caused by pupils?

1.


2.


3.


4.

What tactics from this Activity will you be able to use most often?

## Teachers in Control

◆ **ACTIVITY 2.1** ◆◆◆

Whatever age you teach and in whatever kind of school, you will be aware that teaching is an activity that can be constantly improved and refined. Good teachers, like you, never stand still and rest on their past laurels. They know what they are good at and practise doing this, but they also continue learning new and better techniques.

*Unit 1* was concerned with developing techniques to deal with individual pupils; I will return to a more detailed way of monitoring individual behaviour in the final Unit. This Activity, and subsequent ones in this Unit, will try to establish more general issues which, whilst being equally applicable to individuals, will help you look at the class(es) you teach as a whole.

This Activity is concerned with the following seven aspects of your classroom management:

❖ The taught curriculum
❖ Classroom organisation
❖ Management of pupil activities
❖ Classroom atmosphere
❖ Routines
❖ Teaching strategies
❖ Links between home and school

Read the questions in each section and then respond to the general questions in the spaces.

### 1. The taught curriculum

How broad, balanced, relevant and differentiated is the taught curriculum in your classroom?

Are your assessment and recording systems effective?

Do you understand the content of the curriculum you are teaching?

Are the outcomes you expect in your lessons interesting and varied?

What aspects of these issues are you good at?

What are you less good at and need to develop more?

How are you going to improve these areas? What help do you need?

## 2. Classroom organisation

Does the physical layout of your classroom create a positive learning environment?

Are there enough appropriate resources for you to teach as effectively as you want to teach?

Are the resources to which you have access used well?

Are pupils grouped appropriately for the kind of teaching you want to do?

> What problems with resources and classroom furniture/layout do you have that affects what you can do in your classroom?

## 3. Management of pupil activities

When you are teaching and move from one activity to another, is there a smooth change with little disruption?

Are you able to have 'eyes in the back of your head' and monitor all the activities going on in your classroom?

Are you able to do several things at once?

> What areas of managing pupil activities are you less good at? How will you be able to improve? What help will you get?

## 4. Classroom atmosphere

Does the general classroom ethos promote good behaviour and positive relationships?

Is there an atmosphere of productive interaction between teachers and pupils?

> How do you create an ethos which encourages good relationships?

## 5. Routines

Are there enough formal routines in classrooms to contribute to a well-organised learning environment?

Are the pupils clear about classroom routines and what to do or not to do?

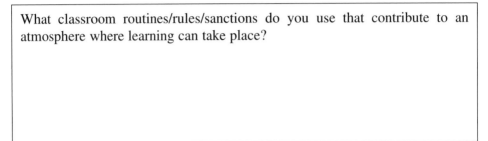

What classroom routines/rules/sanctions do you use that contribute to an atmosphere where learning can take place?

## 6. Teaching strategies

Do you use teaching strategies which promote clear learning responses?

Have you the necessary skills to use if pupils are not responding appropriately?

List some of the skills that you would use as part of your teaching strategies.

## 7. Links between home and school

How do you establish links between home and school?

Are there enough useful links between home and school that will help in the teaching and learning process in your classroom?

What kind of communication is used to improve the links between home and school?

How do you promote good home-school links that help with your classroom discipline?

What do you need to improve in your home-school links?

## ◆ ACTIVITY 2.2 ◆◆◆

In *Activity 2.1*, there were seven aspects of classroom management that you were asked to consider and respond to. Now you are going to look at some case studies. They are as realistic as possible and should help you to relate to and use many more areas of teaching and control. As well as using your responses from *Activity 2.1*, the questions beneath the case studies are based on Appendix B: Factors associated with better classroom practice in the survey schools (pp.22–23) in *Curriculum Organisation and Classroom Practice in Primary Schools: A Follow-up Report* (OFSTED, 1993). The criteria used apply equally to teaching in secondary schools, so they can be used by teachers of all age ranges. The headings used by OFSTED include:

— organisational strategies;
— teaching techniques;
— teachers' knowledge.

Read *Case study A* and the questions that follow it. Then respond in the spaces provided.

Bear in mind that you are trying to identify your areas of strength and weakness. When you give your responses, you might like to consider, for example, whether you are skilful or not at giving oral instructions, providing opportunities for pupils to answer questions and organising the class to work in groups.

So, as well as dealing directly with the case study and its specific questions, try to suggest what you can do successfully and what you are less effective at doing.

Repeat this for each case study.

## Case study A

You have prepared quite a lengthy lesson that lasts for 90 minutes. It involves starting and finishing all the work in the time allowed. You want the class to work in pairs for some of the time but to do much of the written work on their own. Everyone seems to understand what to do and you have made sure that, in your lesson plans, you know that pupils with different abilities will produce different outcomes.

If the lesson is to last 1½ hours, how will you divide the time between individual, pair, group and whole class teaching?

How will you break up the time to include: time for giving instructions, teaching the whole class, individuals, pairs and groups and moving between activities to instruct, question, explain and assess?

## Case study B

You have arranged a visit to a local farm. It is the day before the visit. You are explaining to the class/group some of the details of the visit. The explanation includes what work they are expected to do, what they have to look for and the major points about behaviour.

| Why is it important to give good oral instruction? |
| --- |
| What opportunities would you give for pupils to ask questions? |
| What kinds of questions might you ask that could encourage pupils to think carefully about the visit? |

## Case study C

You are in your classroom in mid-lesson. The pupils are in the middle of the work that you have set. You want to assess some of them but are conscious that several pupils don't really understand what they are supposed to be doing. Others are not working particularly well and some have nearly finished.

| |
|---|
| How will you intervene in the lesson to make sure that everyone is involved and learning? |
| How can you use some of the work by pupils to encourage others? |
| How will you target specific pupils? |
| How will you arrange to assess some of the pupils? |

## Case study D

You are in the middle of a lesson, everyone is working well and you have time to look around the classroom and pause for thought. You decide that, as everyone is busy and pupils of all abilities are getting something out of the lesson, you will use the work the pupils are doing for assessment. As you walk round the room talking to individuals, you realise that the outcomes are really good but, for some reason, some of them are very different from those you expected.

How would it have helped if you had made the criteria for assessing work more explicit to the pupils?

How do you make sure, in cases like these, that you have a good knowledge of the pupils' current levels of achievement and the level to which they should be progressing?

*Is this the right time to assess work?*

♦ **ACTIVITY 2.3** ♦♦♦

This whole Unit recognises that one of the most important aspects of teaching is control. You have to be in control so that you can work out your own repertoire of strategies to make sure that, in controlling the classes you teach, you are able to enhance your pupils' learning experiences.

Here are some actual *Methods of classroom control.*

Read each one and, in the space beneath each one, write down:

— when you have used this method;
— whether it had the desired effect;
— in what circumstances you used it;
— if you haven't used it, why you haven't.

## Methods of Classroom Control

*Control by being in authority*

This method is considered to be the traditional way by which teachers manage their classrooms. They take most, if not all, decisions and teach by telling rather than by explaining or justifying what they are doing. This kind of control is associated with strictness and formality, both in how the teacher teaches and how the classroom is actually arranged. It is possible to see authority of this kind as repressive and depriving pupils of exercising any choice.

*Control by being permissive*

This is often seen as being the opposite of authoritarian control but it is important to recognise it as 'more' permissive, not permissive bordering on anarchic. By using this method, teachers give fewer instructions, adopt a more flexible style, and create an atmosphere which allows choice and expects pupils to take some responsibility for their own actions.

*Control through successful relationships*

The teacher who uses this method tries to create a classroom atmosphere where learning will develop through good relationships between teacher and pupils and between pupils. There may well be a policy where all pupils in the class are asked their opinions, and rules and working patterns may be negotiated.

*Control by changing behaviour*

This is a method used by teachers who believe that good behaviour needs celebrating or reinforcing and misbehaviour should, where possible, be ignored. There may well be a system of positive rewards for good behaviour and those whose bad behaviour is ignored, as far as it is possible to ignore disruptions, could be involved in behaviour contracts (see *Unit 5*) where their good and bad deeds are monitored on a daily or weekly basis.

*Tactical control*

This method uses tactics, techniques and skills that are learned through experience. This experience has taught the teacher to look for certain signs and react accordingly. For example, s/he learns to spot misbehaviour in its early stages rather than when it becomes very disruptive; to work with a small group and, at the same time, monitor the whole class; to avoid spending too long on any area so that it becomes boring; and to show pupils that s/he is interested in them and is well aware of what they are actually doing during lessons.

*Control by knowing the class and the pupils*

This method acknowledges that it is important to know the details of the pupils that are taught. This can involve understanding social and financial conditions, religion, diet, beliefs, etc. and accepting that sometimes external factors may impinge on what you are able to do in the classroom.

# ◆ ACTIVITY 2.4 ◆◆◆

In *Activity 2.3* you will have written down your responses about whether you used certain methods of control, the effect it had and in what circumstances you used it.

It should become obvious that no one method is at the top of any control hierarchy, nor is one so useless that it should never be used.

All of them should be used in certain circumstances and all of them will work. In fact many situations will demand the use of a mixture of methods of classroom control.

This Activity consists of some extremely realistic *Case studies*.

Read each one and in the spaces suggest:

— which method(s) of control from *Activity 2.3* you would use;
— whether there is a main method and whether there are other subsidiary ones;
— what else you might need to do or know in order to control the situation.

## Case study 1

There is one pupil in your class or tutor group who hits someone else in the class/group almost every day. S/he has recently taken to doing it at the same time as verbally abusing the other pupil. The kinds of things said are very hurtful and, depending on whom s/he is hitting can be sexist and/or racist.

## Case study 2

Two boys have arrived in your class on Monday morning after a shop-lifting spree. They are selling a collection of pens, rulers and rubbers to other pupils.

## Case study 3

You are talking to the whole class. One girl is messily blowing bubbles with bubble gum and bursting them loudly.

## Case study 4

It is the beginning of a lesson and the class you are about to teach begins to rush into the room, trampling on each other's bags and pushing and jostling.

## Case study 5

It is the beginning of the school year. One of the classes you are teaching has four girls in it who spend half their time giggling and the rest of the time swearing quietly at anyone who comes near them. They often look round the room for approval from their peers.

## Case study 6

You have just finished a lesson and it is time to put all the books, equipment and apparatus away. You tell the class what to do and, after a few minutes, you find that only a few girls and no boys are clearing up. Most of the boys are waiting near the door for a quick getaway when the bell for the end of the lesson goes.

◆ **ACTIVITY 2.5** ◆◆◆

As a final Activity, let's quickly and briefly summarise your control tactics, remembering that being in control is important.

Complete the *Control action plan*.

## Control Action Plan

| |
|---|
| What control tactics will you use in the future which you need to develop more? |
| What control tactics are you already good at? |

What control tactics are you poor at and need to learn?

How will you learn these tactics you aren't very good at and who will help you?

# UNIT 3

## Beginnings

When people meet for the first time or after a considerable interval, a great deal of information needs to be shared. Each person tries to find out about the other; whether they like the same things or share the same views, whether they are from the same background or have similar intelligence, whether they like each other and, if it is in the professional context of an interview, whether they could work together.

Similar exchanges happen between teachers and pupils, including mutual appraisal. It is in every teacher's interest to make an impact when first meeting a teaching group, or becoming reacquainted with a class or tutor group after a holiday. It is also important to make a good impression each time you teach a group.

In other words, every day and every lesson is a time for a good, professional and effective beginning.

Diane Montgomery in *Managing Behaviour Problems* (Hodder and Stoughton, 1989) suggests, in a section headed 'Personal Presentation in the Classroom' (p.19), that there are facial expressions that teachers use which can influence how the group or class reacts.

The meeting-of-friends smile is an open-faced direct gaze, with mouth slightly open showing upper teeth only, tilt at corners of mouth and eyes and crowsfeet wrinkles. The chin is tilted slightly upwards and small bags are produced under each eye by the lifting action of the face muscles. The eyebrows are quickly raised and dropped in recognition. This kind of first meeting smile tells everyone that you like them and that they should feel significant.

The not-sure-that-I-can-cope smile is a fixed smile showing upper teeth, thin lower lip pulled in, upper teeth almost over lower lip as though biting, head down, eyes looking up slightly to the side, rather shyly. This smile signifies unsureness, submission and anxiety to the onlooker and suggests a scared individual.

It is important to enter any teaching situation with a firm tread, head up, chin tilted slightly forward, shoulders back and an easy, confident pose. If you can emanate such feelings of confidence, it should be easy to create a pleasant, positive and supportive classroom atmosphere.

## ◆ ACTIVITY 3.1 ◆◆◆

Let's start with the beginning of the school year and establish some broad beginnings before looking more closely at how good you are at the beginning of lessons.

List some of the things you do or say to your pupils at the beginning of the school year that are intended to establish the kind of control you want.

### Beginning of the School Year Sheet

| What do you do or say? | What effect does it have? |
|---|---|
| 1. | |
| 2. | |
| 3. | |
| 4. | |
| 5. | |
| 6. | |
| 7. | |
| 8. | |

*The beginning of the year.*

♦ **ACTIVITY 3.2** ♦♦♦

Before moving on to the beginnings of lessons, let's establish a few more details about the beginning of the year when you first meet a new teaching group.

Quickly read what you have written in *Activity 3.1*. Now let's explore the kind of beginning you want in slightly more detail. Write your responses in the spaces.

| |
|---|
| Is there one thing, or several things, that you always do at the beginning of each year? If so, why? |
| Is arriving early in the classroom important? Why? |

Are there such things as the beginning-of-the-year clothes that suggest authority?

What kind of pre-year planning is important?

◆ **ACTIVITY 3.3** ◆◆◆

I think that clothes do matter and can be a means of control *if* they are part of good teaching techniques and a considerable amount of planning and preparation.

Professionals need to look and behave as professionals, but, as well as looking the part, having a confident posture and an in-control smile, the first spoken words and the gestures that accompany them are extremely important.

Let's assume that a beginning, that is the *immediate* starting point and your first contact with the class, lasts approximately five minutes. It is the time for settling everyone down, checking that pupils and resources are in place and giving the introductory remarks in your lesson introduction.

Think back to a really wonderful lesson, or think forward to how you are going to begin your most amazing lesson of all time. In the five minutes you are going to use for the beginning, you will have to make several statements, *but*, they don't exist on their own. They have to be accompanied by some body movement and you will be making specific statements in order to achieve something.

Read my example and then complete the *Matching voice and body chart* for yourself, using a good lesson you have had or one that you intend to have in the future.

| |
|---|
| *Opening statement:*<br>OK! Are you all ready? Right, let's make a start. |
| *Body movement:*<br>Standing formally at the front, upright, slight smile, looking precisely round the classroom, especially at those who are obviously paying less attention. |
| *What it should achieve*:<br>It should announce my presence and begin the quietening down process ready to start the lesson straight away. |

Now you try it. There are spaces for up to five statements.

## Matching Voice and Body Chart

| |
|---|
| *Opening statement*: |
| *Body movement*: |
| *What it should achieve*: |
| *Statement 2*: |
| *Body movement*: |
| *What it should achieve*: |

| |
|---|
| *Statement 3*: |
| *Body movement*: |
| *What it should achieve*: |

| |
|---|
| *Statement 4*: |
| *Body movement*: |
| *What it should achieve*: |

| |
|---|
| *Statement 5*: |
| *Body movement*: |
| *What it should achieve*: |

## ♦ ACTIVITY 3.4 ♦♦♦

It will be useful to try and use some of your tactics for beginning lessons on some real life situations, or at least, as near real life as I can imagine.

This Activity consists of two case studies of the beginnings of lessons. They are not unreal and they could have happened in your school recently. What I have done is link various incidents together into one particular lesson. Hopefully, no one should ever find all these things happening at once.

Read *Case study 1* and, as you are reading it, put numbers alongside the points where you would do something, say something or take some kind of action. These are your intervention points.

When you have finished reading *Case study 1* and have numbered all the necessary points, write down on the *Intervention chart for case study 1* what exactly the intervention is, i.e. what you do or say and why you are doing it at this particular point.

It is important to remember that what you are trying to do is to be effective at the beginning of the lesson, i.e. during the first five minutes.

When you have finished this, repeat the whole process for *Case study 2*.

## Case study 1

You are in the classroom first thing in the morning, waiting for the class you teach to arrive. When they come into the room, they are noisy and push their way through the door, talking loudly to each other. During the first half minute, several pupils get things out of their bags and talk loudly to their immediate neighbours. On one occasion, there is a conversation between two of them from one side of the room to the other. When you are explaining what to do, several pupils haven't got the right equipment, lost or forgotten pencils and pens being the most common items. When you expect them to start work at the end of your introduction, it is obvious that some of them still do not know what they are expected to do. Once they have all started to be on-task, you eventually find, five minutes into the lesson, that three pupils are discussing the plot of last night's soap on television.

### Intervention Chart for Case Study 1

| Number | What you did or said and what you expected to happen |
|--------|------------------------------------------------------|
| 1. | |
| 2. | |
| 3. | |

| 4. | |
|---|---|
| 5. | |
| 6. | |
| 7. | |
| 8. | |
| 9. | |
| 10. | |

## Case study 2

You are beginning a maths lesson. As you begin, one pupil is moving his chair backwards and forwards and another is moving across the room to talk to a friend. When you ask a question, several pupils shout out answers and it is obvious that, whilst some know the answer, others are giving you completely ridiculous ones. A shy girl, whom you eventually ask for the answer, is jeered at by a group of vociferous boys. When you give out some of the equipment they need, two pupils snatch it out of each other's hands and knock some of it on the floor. Each time one of the class shouts out an answer, s/he grins and looks at his/her friends. When you ask them to begin the calculations in their books, some of them are writing with pencils and some with pens. Their general presentation is appalling and it is obvious that some don't understand the questions in the text book. The books have to be shared, one book between two pupils. Some do not seem to be able to share at all sensibly.

### Intervention Chart for Case Study 2

| Number | What you did or said and what you expected to happen |
|--------|------------------------------------------------------|
| 1. | |
| 2. | |
| 3. | |

| | |
|---|---|
| 4. | |
| 5. | |
| 6. | |
| 7. | |
| 8. | |
| 9. | |
| 10. | |

## ◆ **ACTIVITY 3.5** ◆◆◆

This Unit has been concerned with how you start teaching a group or class of pupils.

Before you complete the *Final action plan*, read each of the absolutely essential ways, listed below, that teachers need to behave with any class of pupils.

Write down how you manage to be like this and then complete your *Final action plan*.

| FIRM: by controlling the pupils without being too punitive. |
|---|
| How do you do it? |
| |
| FAIR: by consistently being perceived as fair in the sense that only the wrongdoers get punished and there are never any blanket punishments. |
| How do you do it? |
| |
| CONSISTENT: by creating a well-organised atmosphere with plenty of recognised praise. |
| How do you do it? |
| |

ABLE TO TEACH: by explaining well so that work gets done and pupils feel that they are making progress.

How do you do it?

RESPECTFUL: by treating all pupils equally and allowing them to retain their dignity. This kind of teacher usually receives respect in return.

How do you do it?

FRIENDLY: by being amicable without being over-familiar.

How do you do it?

SUPPORTIVE: by helping pupils to achieve good results and praising them for their efforts.

How do you do it?

*A teacher needs to be supportive.*

## Final Action Plan

| Beginnings that I am good at: |
| --- |
| Beginnings that I would like to be good at and only need a little more practice with: |

# UNIT 4
## Establishing Working Rules and Relationships

All classes, in whatever school, have their rules and routines. They can be legislative rules relating to Health and Safety, whole school rules emanating from the headteacher or your own rules and routines that you have established in your classroom in order to create the kinds of behaviour and relationships you want.

Some of these rules will be written down and others will have been created over a period of time by processes of negotiation. At the same time, there will also be instant rules where, after an unexpected event, a rule or routine is created that should prevent it from happening again.

Whatever rules you have in your classroom, most of them will be necessary for high quality teaching and learning to take place. There needs to be a distinction made, however, between those rules and routines which are designed to create an harmonious working atmosphere and those that punish pupils.

The Elton Report (1989) has some important things to say about this distinction: 'Our evidence suggests that schools which put too much faith in punishments to deter bad behaviour are also likely to be disappointed.'

This is also confirmed by research findings. M. Rutter *et al.* in *Fifteen Thousand Hours: Secondary Schools and their Effect on Pupils* (Open Books, 1979), found that different forms or frequencies of punishment bore little or no relationship to standards of behaviour in secondary schools. P. Mortimore *et al.*, in *School Matters: The Junior Years* (Open Books, 1988), found that behaviour tended to be worse in junior schools which emphasised punishments rather than rewards; 'the more punishments listed, the more negative the effect seemed to be' and '. . . punitive regimes seem to be associated with worse rather than better standards of behaviour. This does not mean that punishments are not necessary . . . the message seems to be that, in order to create a positive atmosphere, schools need to establish a healthy balance between punishments and rewards.' (pp.98–99)

◆ **ACTIVITY 4.1**  ◆◆◆

Write down the *five* most important rules in your classroom and, underneath each one, write down why it is important and how the pupils you are teaching know that it is one of your classroom rules.

### Five Important Classroom Rules

| 1. |
|---|
|  |

| 2. |
|---|
|  |

| 3. |
|---|
|  |

| 4. |
|---|
|  |

| 5. |
|---|
|  |

## ◆ ACTIVITY 4.2 ◆◆◆

In the previous Activity, you will have identified five of your important rules. Perhaps you have more, but some rules are more important than others.

If this is the case, you must have plans for what happens if your pupils break these rules and you must recognise that your response affects the classroom relationships.

For each of your five rules from *Activity 4.1*, write your responses in the spaces.

### Classroom Rules Sheet

| Rule | What do you do if it is broken? | How does breaking it affect relationships? |
|------|--------------------------------|--------------------------------------------|
| 1.   |                                |                                            |
| 2.   |                                |                                            |
| 3.   |                                |                                            |

| | | |
|---|---|---|
| 4. | | |
| 5. | | |

## ◆ ACTIVITY 4.3 ◆◆◆

This Activity contains a composite list of classroom rules. Most of them will apply to all schools but there may be the occasional one that is primary- or secondary-specific. If this is the case and the rule really does not apply to your classroom and your school, miss it out.

Read the list of *Important and less important rules*.

In the space after each rule, write down one of the following scores:

       1 . . . If this rule is vitally important
       2 . . . If it is reasonably important
       3 . . . If it is not really important
       4 . . . If it is of no importance whatsoever

### Important and Less Important Rules

*Rules relating to relationships*:

| | |
|---|---|
| 1. Be considerate to other people. | |
| 2. Share and co-operate. | |

| | |
|---|---|
| 3.  Be thoughtful and polite. | |
| 4.  Be well mannered. | |
| 5.  Don't ever hit anyone else. | |
| 6.  Don't ever verbally abuse anyone else. | |
| 7.  Don't ever ridicule anyone else's work. | |

*Rules relating to classroom space*:

| | |
|---|---|
| 1.  Don't go into the classroom at break or during lunchtime without permission. | |
| 2.  Use the classroom for work, not play. | |
| 3.  Don't touch anyone's work when you move from your seat. | |
| 4.  Use the reading corner for reading only. | |

*Rules relating to what pupils wear*:

| | |
|---|---|
| 1. School uniform must be worn at all times. | |
| 2. Ties have to be fastened correctly. | |
| 3. Pullovers must be 'V' necked. | |
| 4. Blazers can only be removed in the summer after a school decision. | |

*Rules relating to equipment and resources*:

| | |
|---|---|
| 1. Put things away when you have used them. | |
| 2. Keep all books tidy. | |
| 3. If you have made a mess on the floor, sweep it up. | |
| 4. Put everything away at the end of the day. | |
| 5. Do not write on desks or book covers. | |
| 6. If you borrow something, return it. | |
| 7. Stack the classroom chairs at the end of each day. | |
| 8. Respect other people's property. | |

*Rules relating to work*:

| | |
|---|---|
| 1. Hand in your work when you are asked. | |
| 2. Make sure that all work is neatly written. | |
| 3. Work on your own quietly and peacefully. | |
| 4. If you are asked to work in a group, do so in an appropriate way. | |
| 5. Never interfere with or distract other people who are working. | |
| 6. Work quietly if the teacher has to leave the room. | |

*Rules relating to noise and talking*:

| | |
|---|---|
| 1. Don't talk when the teacher is talking to the class. | |
| 2. If you are working in a group, talk only about the work you are doing. | |
| 3. Don't talk if another pupil is talking to the class. | |
| 4. Never shout out. | |
| 5. Always put your hand up if you want to answer a question. | |
| 6. Be absolutely silent when the register is being taken. | |

*Rules relating to movement and safety*:

| | |
|---|---|
| 1. Don't run, push or shove in the classroom. | |
| 2. Take care with scissors and other sharp equipment. | |
| 3. Ask, if you want to leave the room. | |
| 4. Don't wander around the room or move from seat to seat. | |
| 5. Don't swing on your chair or move anyone else's chair. | |

*Take care with scissors and other sharp equipment.*

◆ **ACTIVITY 4.4** ◆◆◆

The previous two Activities have identified important and less important rules.

When you are working with your pupils, you need to be able to explain your rules to them in a way that they can understand. How you do this is important, because it is no good expecting your pupils to pick up your rules by a process of osmosis. They will have to be emphasised, reinforced and repeated over and over again.

How successful you are at doing this will influence the kinds of relationships you have with your pupils.

Look back at *Activities 4.1* and *4.2* and this time choose *ten* rules that you think are important. This is just for purposes of recognition, not in order of priority.

Keep your original rules from *Activity 4.1* if you still feel they are absolutely vital but add some more to make *ten* important rules.

1.

2.

3.

4.

5.

6.

7.

8.

9.

10.

Read the suggestions and examples on how to explain rules to pupils on the *Explaining rules sheet*.

In the space alongside each one, write down the number of the rule, from your list of ten, that you would explain in this way.

Some rules can be under more than one heading. Put them under as many headings as you feel is necessary.

## Explaining Rules Sheet

| | |
|---|---|
| *Laying down the law*<br>e.g. 'All those in group 3 stand up and come here. You do not work in a group making that amount of noise. Now go back and work properly and quietly.' | |
| *Giving an explanation*<br>e.g. 'You must put up your chairs so that the cleaner can sweep the floor.' | |
| *Expressing righteous indignation*<br>e.g. 'I am really disappointed in you. Never run with scissors in your hand. You might hurt someone.' | |
| *Generalising*<br>e.g. 'I'd like to see a few more good manners this week, please.' | |
| *Being calmly specific*<br>e.g. 'No one is allowed to shout out. You must put your hands up.' | |
| *Asking general questions*<br>e.g. 'Why is it important to think about putting things away tidily?' | |
| *Negotiating rules*<br>e.g. 'When we are doing technology there are far too many people moving around the room. How can we stop that happening next week?' | |
| *Asking specific questions*<br>e.g. 'Why do I tell people not to push when they come into the classroom?' | |

# ◆ **ACTIVITY 4.5** ◆◆◆

At the beginning of this Unit there was evidence from Elton, Rutter and Mortimore which suggested that a system based on punishments only will be counter-productive.

There needs to be a balance between rewards and punishments and certainly rewards are extremely effective if used appropriately.

There are usually two basic kinds of rewards:

✤ *External rewards:* These are given to a pupil and have usually been earned by him/her. They are often visible like a gold star, a prize in assembly, a comment in a book that is more significant than usual.

✤ *Internal rewards:* These usually come from within and are the feelings of satisfaction when something has been done well. Praise, a smile, a word of encouragement from a teacher can often trigger off a person's internal rewards system.

How do you reward your pupils? Remember, a smile and a nod of encouragement are often important to pupils.

Write down a list of your usual methods of reward.

### **Rewarding Pupils**

| |
|---|
| 1. |
| 2. |
| 3. |

| |
|---|
| 4. |
| 5. |
| 6. |

# ◆ ACTIVITY 4.6 ◆◆◆

Let's try and match some realistic situations to the kinds of reward(s) that might be offered.

Here are some case studies.

Read each one and in the spaces first of all write down what reward you think that you would give.

Secondly, write down why, in other words, what giving this reward would achieve.

Thirdly, suggest how you would give this reward, e.g. quietly after other pupils have left, publicly in the classroom, publicly in assembly.

## Case study 1

One of your pupils, not renowned for her neatness, has just produced a carefully presented piece of English.

| What reward would you give? |
| --- |
| Why would you give this reward? |
| How would you give it? |

## Case study 2

A rather disruptive boy who constantly talks and gossips, distracting other pupils round him, has just finished a piece of work in 45 minutes that other pupils finished half an hour ago.

| What reward would you give? |
| --- |
| Why would you give this reward? |
| How would you give it? |

## Case study 3

A pupil, whom you told off yesterday for shouting out the answers to questions, has just put her hand up twice and given the correct answers.

| What reward would you give? |
|---|
| Why would you give this reward? |
| How would you give it? |

## Case study 4

One of your pupils has just won a painting competition out of school, organised by a local supermarket.

| What reward would you give? |
|---|
| Why would you give this reward? |
| How would you give it? |

**Case study 5**

During a recent mock exam, your pupils have all scored rather highly.

| |
|---|
| What reward would you give? |
| Why would you give this reward? |
| How would you give it? |

◆ **ACTIVITY 4.7** ◆◆◆

As a final Activity look back through the Unit and then complete the *Individual action plan*.

Do it carefully, as it should help you to recognise your strengths and weaknesses.

### Individual Action Plan

| |
|---|
| Rules I find it easy to establish: |
| 1. |
| 2. |
| 3. |
| 4. |
| 5. |

Rules I find it difficult to establish:

1.

2.

3.

4.

5.

Help I will need:

Rewards I use most often:

1.

2.

3.

4.

5.

Rewards I find it difficult to use but would like to try:

1.

2.

3.

4.

5.

Help I will need:

## Setting Behaviour Targets

This is the final Unit and I have written it to help you be aware of ways in which pupils can begin to take some charge of their own behaviour. It contains a number of examples of reports and contracts you can use with individual pupils who are causing you problems in your classroom.

Using them, however, takes time. They are not for the normal, routine types of behaviour that inevitably happen in all classrooms. They are designed to be used when most other tactics have failed, or as part of a series of techniques when you know that the behaviour you are trying to stop is likely to be difficult and long term.

♦ **ACTIVITY 5.1** ♦♦♦

First of all, let's try to identify some of the important and long-term behaviour issues by using the *Problem behaviour identification sheet*. Use it over a period of a week and fill it in with all the general details that it asks for.

*Problem behaviour.*

## Form 1: Problem Behaviour Identification Form

| Description of incident | Where incident took place, e.g. at desk | Time | What pupil was doing at the time | Teacher action |
|---|---|---|---|---|
|  |  |  |  |  |

◆ **ACTIVITY 5.2** ◆◆◆

In previous Activities you have usually been asked to identify different kinds of disruptive incidents and then have gone on to find out what are the most effective solutions.

This time I want you to try a slightly different approach.

Use the *Problem behaviour identification form* in *Activity 5.1* to complete the following:

| |
|---|
| Where do most incidents occur? |
| Is there a time of day when there are more disruptive incidents? |
| Are there common activities that the pupils were doing at the time of the disruptive incident? |

◆ **ACTIVITY 5.3** ◆◆◆

When you have completed *Activities 5.1* and *5.2*, you should have a good idea of what disruptive incidents have been common in your classroom and, to a certain extent, where they occurred and what triggered them off, i.e. what your pupils were doing at the time.

Now that you have this information, look back at previous Units and see whether the rules and rewards you use are still relevant.

Quickly write down what you now regard as *five* absolutely essential classroom rules or behaviour targets. By doing this, by recognising what you need to do, you should be able to begin to reduce incidents to a minimum.

| |
|---|
| 1. |
| 2. |
| 3. |
| 4. |
| 5. |

◆ **ACTIVITY 5.4** ◆◆◆

What happens in your classroom is not just dependent on your individual skills. It relies to some extent on whole school support, consistency between classes and teachers and a certain amount of backing from other staff, pupils and parents. In other words, pupils have to be aware of the constraints placed on them and be able to behave appropriately. *Form 2: Personal disruption identification form* is meant to be used with an individual pupil.

Select a pupil you have identified on *Form 1* and complete *Form 2* with him/her. This will not be able to be completed instantly because of the section needing parent's comments; in fact you *must* involve and talk to parents during the completion of this form. When you have finished it, complete the questions that follow it.

## Form 2: Personal Disruption Identification Form

| | |
|---|---|
| *Name*:................................................................ *Class*:............................ | |

*What I did*: (Describe incident in your own words.)

*What rule I know I broke*:

*Why I did it*: (Describe this in your own words.)

*What I should do to prevent myself from doing it again*:

*What I should do to apologise to other people*:

*Teacher's comments*:

*Parent's comments*:

*What follow-up is needed*:

*Signed* (pupil): ...............................................................

*Signed* (teacher): ...............................................................

*Signed* (parent): ...............................................................

| Is it beneficial to ask disruptive pupils to complete sections of the form? If so, why? |
|---|
| What effect might it have on future behaviour? |
| Why do you think that it is important to ask pupils to explain why they behaved badly or why they did what they did? |
| How important is it to involve parents in completing such a form? |

# ◆ **ACTIVITY 5.5** ◆◆◆

*Form 2* is, in essence, a collaboration between the disruptive pupil, you as the teacher and the parent. *Form 3: Behaviour monitoring form*, is for the pupil to use to monitor his/her own behaviour and for you to use as a tool for discussing what it is that the pupil is doing.

The form is designed to be used on a daily basis. It is more difficult to use than others because it requires you to monitor what the pupil is writing on it every hour. If the pupil goes to other lessons with other teachers, they must be able and willing to carry on using the form.

Read through the instructions with the pupil, explain the symbols to be used and tell him/her that you, or another teacher, are going to comment on what has been written every hour.

It might be useful to give some examples of good and bad behaviour so that the pupil has some idea about what to write. For example, shouting out without putting up hand is 'bad', while sticking to the task without wandering around the room is 'good'. In addition, make sure that if you or any other teacher see the pupil doing something that needs recording, you will tell him/her.

A further addition to this form is to suggest rewards, e.g. four 'goods' and only one 'bad' means that you can . . . (You must think of a reward that is suitable to the pupil's age and needs.)

*Rewarding the pupil.*

In practical terms this kind of close monitoring is time consuming, but, if you want to work with a pupil and modify his//her behaviour, it is worth trying. After all, it is only appropriate with a limited number of pupils and you would *never* be using this form for more than two pupils at any one time.

If you feel that you should be using it for many more, perhaps you should be questioning some of your other techniques.

You can recognise if this method is working if there are more positive comments than negative ones. If the number of negative ones remains the same, it is advisable to think of another strategy.

## Form 3: Behaviour Monitoring Form

*Instructions:*

There are approximately three hours in the morning and two in the afternoon, i.e. five hours. The form is divided into five spaces. *Think* how you are behaving and every time you know you are doing well write it down. Do the same if you behave badly.

Mark it VG for Very Good; G for Good; B for Bad and VB for Very Bad. *You* decide what to write unless your teacher tells you to write something.

At the end of every hour, take it to your teacher and s/he will add a comment. At the end of the day *you must discuss it with your teacher before you go home*.

| Name: .......................................................... Class/Form: ............................. |||
|---|---|---|
| **How I behaved** | **Mark** | **Teacher comment** |
| e.g. I swore at Mark. | VB | |
| | | |
| | | |
| | | |
| | | |

◆ **ACTIVITY 5.6** ◆◆◆

The next form, *Form 4: Pupil/teacher/parent contract*, is a more formal contract between the pupil, the teacher and the parent. It involves preparation and discussion with all three. This will mean that you will have to be able and prepared to set aside time for these meetings. When such a meeting is set up, it is important that the bad behaviour that the pupil has agreed to try to correct has been clearly identified. The teacher must take the lead in deciding this, although it is useful and diplomatic to allow some negotiation if pupil and parent are able to put forward their views.

During the discussion, it is important to complete the section on the form headed: *Good behaviour that will replace it*. This also gives you, the teacher, an opportunity to restate what is or is not acceptable behaviour. What you suggest for this section needs to be in the form of small but precise steps, e.g. 'I will try and stay sitting down.'

The *Daily comments* should last for five days before the contract is reviewed with the pupil. Involve the parents again if you have to, but don't feel that it is essential. Before using *Form 4* consider and respond to these questions:

| |
|---|
| How would you organise discussions between the pupil, you and the parent(s)? |
| Where would you hold them? |
| When would they take place? |
| What kind of teacher help will you be able to give to pupils who are making an effort with a contract of this kind? |

## Form 4: Pupil/Teacher/Parent Contract

| |
|---|
| *Pupil's name*:................................. *Teacher's name*:.................................. |
| *Bad behaviour that needs changing*: |
| *Good behaviour that will replace it*: |
| *Teacher help that is needed*: |
| *Parent help that is needed*: |
| *Daily comments*:<br>*Day 1* |
| *Day 2* |
| *Day 3* |
| *Day 4* |
| *Day 5* |
| *Signed* (pupil): .............................................................<br>*Signed* (teacher): .........................................................<br>*Signed* (parent): ......................................................... |

# ◆ ACTIVITY 5.7 ◆◆◆

This handbook has been concerned with improving your classroom control and discipline. I hope it has succeeded and that you feel more confident, skilful and effective.

Use this last Activity as your final celebration of both what you have learned and been able to develop and how you intend to tackle the difficulties of teaching when you go into your classroom tomorrow morning.

## Action Plan

List *six* ways you will tackle whole class control and discipline.

List *six* ways you will tackle the control and discipline of individual pupils in your classroom.

# Further Reading

Alexander, R., Rose, J. and Woodhead, C., *Curriculum Organisation and Classroom Practice in Primary Schools* (DES, 1992)

Bennett, N. *et al.*, *The Quality of Pupils' Learning Experience* (LEA, London, 1984)

Elton *et al.*, *Report of the Committee of Enquiry: Discipline in Schools* (HMSO, 1989)

HMI, *Education in England 1990-91: The Annual Report of HM Senior Inspector of Schools* (DES, 1992)

Montgomery, D., *Managing Behaviour Problems* (Hodder and Stoughton, London, 1989)

Mortimore, P. *et al.*, *School Matters: The Junior Years* (Open Books, Wells, 1988)

Rogers, B., *You know the Fair Rule* (Longman, London, 1991)

Rutter, M. *et al.*, *Fifteen Thousand Hours: Secondary Schools and their Effect on Pupils* (Open Books, Wells, 1979)

Saunders, M., *Class Control and Behaviour Problems* (McGraw-Hill, New York, 1979)

Smith, R., 'What makes a good teacher', *Child Education* (December 1988)

Smith, R., 'Fail proof policy: raising children's self esteem', *Child Education* (May 1990)

Smith, R., *The Effective School, Volume 2: Classroom Techniques and Management* (Framework Press, Lancaster, 1990)

Smith, R., *Managing Pupil Behaviour in School and Classroom: In-house Training Materials for Teachers* (Framework Press, Lancaster, 1993)

Smith, R., *Managing Your Classroom: A Guide to Better Teaching* (Framework Press, Lancaster, 1994)

Solity, J. and Raybould, B., *A Teacher's Guide to Special Needs* (OUP, Oxford, 1988)

Wragg, E, C., *Classroom Teaching Skills* (Croom Helm, London, 1984)